TEN STEPS TO
BRINGING YOUR
Vision TO PASS

UNIVERSAL MINISTRIES

DR. ANNMARIE McQUEEN, TH.D.

Dear Reader

Everyone needs vision. Vision can take on many forms. It depends on the phase of life an individual happens to be in or the situation of life an individual is faced with.

Vision offers direction, clarity and boundaries. It offers direction for the **where,** clarity for the **how** and boundaries for the **path** to be taken. Dear reader, if you have a vision of what you want out of life, you can follow the path that leads to the vision. If you have no vision, life can become chaotic. You might end up following many paths but all of them leading to nowhere in particular.

Psalms 29:19a says:

Where there is no vision, the people perish, (KJV)

Where there is no vision the people cast off restraint; (JPS)

Without a vision is a people made naked, (YLT)

Where there is no vision, the people are uncontrolled; (BBE)

When prophecy shall fail, the people shall be scattered abroad; (DRB)

Where there is no prophetic vision the people cast off restraint; (ESV)

Some think of a vision as something mystical that is only needed by the Pastor for the congregation. However, a teenager might have a vision to finish high school and go on to a particular college. With that in mind he can work towards the goal or vision. A young woman might have a vision for a career or a young man for business, an auxiliary leader might have a vision for the Ushers, Minister of Music for the Praise Team, etc. Whatever the case, what is important is to at least have a plan and an execution plan.

In this book we will examine Abraham's vision. He desired to see his son marry within the family. The family, however, was in a faraway place the Lord had commanded him to leave. How would he accomplish what he wanted to see come to pass? He passed his vision on to his servant. The servant caught the vision and Abraham's vision became his vision and assignment.

Ten Steps to Bringing Your Vision to Pass

Copyright © 2004 by McQueen Universal Ministries

2nd edition (c) 2017

mcqueenum@gmail.com

TEN STEPS TO BRINGING YOUR VISION TO PASS

FROM

GENESIS 24

BY

DR. ANNMARIE MCQUEEN, TH. D

Table of Contents
Genesis 24

Introduction

In Genesis 24, we find an incredible passage. It is the story of Abraham sending his servant to his country and among his kindred to find a wife for Abraham's son, Isaac. In the story, the name of Abraham's servant is not mentioned. All we know of him is that he was his oldest servant. I dare say he was probably his most trusted servant as well since he had rule over all that Abraham had, which was a lot. We know that Abraham had a lot because in verse one of the same chapter as well as chapter 13, verse 2, the Bible says, "*Abram was very rich...*"

The story unfolds with Abraham, who is now very old, calling his servant to swear concerning his desire and vision. Abraham had a desire or vision that he wanted to see come to pass. He was going to work through his oldest servant to bring his vision to pass. Walk with me through Genesis 24 and look at each point, not only naturally but also spiritually. The Lord has a desire and vision for you, for His church and for the whole earth. If you are His, then it is through you that He wants to bring His desire and vision to pass. In heaven, His will is being carried out perfectly. He wants it done on the earth as well (Matthew 6:10). It is to our benefit to bring the plan and vision of our Master and Father to pass.

"For I know the plans I have for you, declares the LORD, plans for welfare and not for evil, to give you a future and a hope." Jeremiah 29:11 (ESV).

Chapter 1

Receive Instruction

Genesis 24:2-8

2 *And Abraham said unto his eldest servant of his house, that ruled over all that he had, Put, I pray thee, thy hand under my thigh:*

3 *And I will make thee swear by the LORD, the God of heaven, and the God of the earth, that thou shalt not take a wife unto my son of the daughters of the Canaanites, among whom I dwell:*

4 *But thou shalt go unto my country, and to my kindred, and take a wife unto my son Isaac.*

5 *And the servant said unto him, Peradventure the woman will not be willing to follow me unto this land: must I needs bring thy son again unto the land from whence thou camest?*

6 *And Abraham said unto him, Beware thou that thou bring not my son thither again.*

7 *The LORD God of heaven, which took me from my father's house, and from the land of my kindred, and which spake unto me, and that sware unto me, saying, Unto thy seed will I give this land; he shall send his angel before thee, and thou shalt take a wife unto my son from thence.*

8 *And if the woman will not be willing to follow thee, then thou shalt be clear from this my oath: only bring not my son thither again.*

The servant is instructed to go and take a wife for Isaac from Abraham's old country and family. He is instructed not to take Isaac's wife from among the Canaanites. He is instructed not to bring Isaac back to his "old country" to marry, in case the woman refuses to travel. He is told that he would be cleared from the oath if the woman will not follow him back to Isaac.

The instructions were clear. He knew exactly what Abraham required of him. He knew his master's desire. He knew what he must do and must not do. Often, we have a vision but it is not clear what we should or should not do. We must be able to define our vision.

Vision here is a *plan* or *desire*. Again, it could be for a specific season or phase in life or for a specific situation. It could also be more broad, it could be for life. To be more precise, it is the "thing" that *you* have seen yourself do with your spiritual eye and that you long to bring into manifestation. It is a part of your destiny. God has shown it to you, you believe it, and you see it, want it, can taste it, and hunger for it. You have known for years that you were born for this but the *how* has escaped you for a long time... until now...

We must do what the servant did here - ask, question, get clarity.

In Dr. Myles Munroe's "Principles and Power of Vision",[1] he writes, "It has been said that if you don't know where you're going, any road will take you there. What's worse, you won't even know when you have arrived." While teaching on this point, the Holy Spirit gave it to me like this, "If you don't know where you are going, any bus will get you there and when you come to your stop, you will not get off the bus." The night I taught this, I had been running late for Bible Study. As a result, I was driving with urgency. I noticed every red light and every slow-moving vehicle in front of me. On one particular road, I noticed that one car would speed up and then slow down and then speed up and slow down and speed up and slow down. I wondered what the driver was doing. I realized that he slowed at each intersection, looked down the road as if to turn, only to speed up past each one. This went on for some time. He found where he was going, I guess, because he finally turned. The Lord showed me something that night. When you do not know where you are going, you will hesitate to go forward. Some people have been hesitating for years. Some people have stopped looking. They do not even know they should be looking. They just "drive" or live aimlessly. They have no idea why they are here. The original reason was clear. In the church, it goes like this... repent, get baptized, and Holy Ghost-filled. Ok, now that we have accomplished that task, now what? Is there anything else? Why are you here, do you know? What is God's plan for your life? Have you sought any instructions? If you have sought God and have received instruction, then read on. If not, stop here and **let us pray**:

---

[1] Dr. Myles Munroe, The Principles and Power of Vision, Keys to achieving personal and corporate Destiny; Whitaker House, 2003, p. 24 (ISBN 0-88368-951-0) www.whitakerhouse.com, bfmadmin@bfmmm.com

Lord Jesus, please reveal to me the plan that You have for my life. According to Jeremiah 29:11, there is an expected end that You have in mind for me. Reveal that to me. Lord, show me Your will and Your way. Clarify the vision to me, Lord, so that I can write it.

Habakkuk 2:2 *And the Lord answered me, and said, Write the vision, and make it plain upon tables, that he may run that readeth it.*

See also

Psalms 27:11 *Teach me thy way, O Lord, and lead me in a plain path, because of mine enemies.*

Psalms 67:2 *That thy way may be known upon earth, thy saving*

health among all nations.

Psalms 143:10 *Teach me to do thy will; for thou art my God: thy spirit*

is good; lead me into the land of uprightness.

Chapter 2

Come Into Agreement (Verse 9)

Genesis 24:9 *"And the servant put his hand under the thigh of Abraham his master, and sware to him concerning the matter."*

You have received instructions. You know what is expected and have direction. Do you agree to go on? Will you accept the challenge. The servant put his hand under Abraham's thigh as a sign of covenanting or agreeing with him that he was accepting his assignment. He knew what he had to do and based on Abraham's word that his God would go with him, he was able to agree to go forward.

Luke 14:26-27 *"If any man come to me, and hate not his father, mother, and wife, and children, and brethren, and sisters, yea, and his own life also, he cannot be my disciple. And whosoever doth not bear his cross, and come after me, cannot be my disciple."*

Some people's salvation plan is not even working out for them, for although they want to be saved they are not willing to agree to the terms of the 'contract'. They, therefore, stumble or hesitate at every turn. They do not live or walk in victory. They are broke, sick, depressed, and always need to be delivered. They go from conference to conference and even from church to church. They always need 'a word' to take them through until the next week. What is the problem? They are not willing to agree to the terms: "I must take up my cross." I have a cross. A cross can be heavy but Jesus is a Burden-bearer. A cross can carry pain but He is a *balm*. A cross can involve persecution but through Him we are all overcomers. The list goes on and on.

Proverbs 13:4 tells us, *"the sluggard desires but has nothing, but the soul of the diligent shall be made fat."* This tells me that desire alone is not enough. We must put feet to our vision. Proverbs 20:4 tells us, *"the sluggard will not plow by reason of the cold; therefore shall he beg in harvest, and have nothing."* The sluggard man or woman never gets anywhere in life. They are all talk and no action. They want what others have but they do not want to DO what others have done to achieve their goals. They are the ones in the church who want the preacher to lay hands on them and give them what they have... they are convinced that it will all just fall on them... Whether in the church or in the market place or at home or in your own personal life, achievement takes work. God has done His part. We must do our part.

Coming into agreement could mean realizing that in order to bring the vision to pass it will mean giving up some things, often precious things and sometimes even *all.*

Read **Luke 14:28-32**

28 For which of you, intending to build a tower, sitteth not down first, and counteth the costs, whether he have sufficient to finish it?

29 Lest haply, after he hath laid the foundation, and is not able to finish it, all that behold it begin to mock him,

30 Saying, This man began to build, and was not able to finish.

31 Or what king, going to make war against another king, sitteth not down first, and consulteth whether he be able with ten thousand to meet him that cometh against him with twenty thousand?

32 Or else, while the other is yet a great way off, he sendeth an ambassage, and desireth conditions of peace.

Verse 33 says, "*So likewise, whosoever he be of you that forsaketh not all that he hath, he cannot be my disciple.*"

Sometimes, coming into agreement could mean coming into covenant with God. What did God promise? If God promised it, you can rest assured that He will bring it to pass. No matter how it looks, hold on to the Word of God and His promise to you. He will never break covenant.

What about others? Are there others with whom you need to agree? Amos 3:3 says, "*Can two walk together, except they be agreed?*" Do you agree that you both want the same thing and are going in the same direction? Often, we find married couples faced with this dilemma. They no longer agree to 'walk' in the same direction. One or both has broken covenant; maybe they did not count up the cost first or maybe they are not willing to give all. There could be many reasons. As you go forth, consider and reconsider who is 'going' with you on this journey. Do you agree? Do they agree? There must be agreement! Once there has been agreement, then full speed ahead. No turning back now. Whatever it takes, however long it takes, there will be no turning back.

Chapter 3

Realize There are Resources at Your Disposal (Verse 10)

Genesis 24:10 *"And the servant took ten camels of the camels of his master, and departed; for all the goods of his master were in his hand: and he arose, and went to Mesopotamia, unto the city of Nahor."*

The servant simply took what he would need for the journey. We do not see where he asked Abraham what to take or how much or if he could take. He took.

Luke 10:19, *"Behold, I give unto you power to tread on serpents and scorpions, and over all the power of the enemy: and nothing shall by any means harm you."* ... Authority. Ability. God has given us authority to use His name and ability through His Word and by the power of the Holy Ghost.

It has been said, "when He calls you, He equips you." Proverbs 8:12 says, *"I wisdom dwell with prudence, and find out knowledge of witty inventions."* By the wisdom of God and the power of the Holy Ghost, God gives us creative ability. We can invent things or come up with ideas. What we need to bring our vision to pass has been provided *in* us by the Lord. When someone else's help is needed, He provides that too. He will give you favor in the eyes of even your enemies to make sure you have what you need in order to do what needs to be done.

See **Exodus 12:35-36**:

> 35 *And the children of Israel did according to the word of Moses; and they borrowed of the Egyptians jewels of silver, and jewels of gold, and raiment:*

> 36 *And the LORD gave the people favour in the sight of the Egyptians, so that they lent unto them such things as they required. And they spoiled the Egyptians.*

All of us have been given certain gifts and talents. Some of us have gifts we have never used. Some of us have gifts we use in our everyday lives. If we tapped into them with purpose, these same everyday "tasks" would take us very far. We must pay attention. "What do you have in your hand?", the Lord asked Moses. He had a piece of stick. He used it to perform miracles, by the power of God. The Lord asked me once, "What do you have in your hand, Annmarie?" I thought of Moses. I thought long and hard. I can teach, Lord. I can write, Lord... The list went on. He told me to use what was in my hand. I was in Germany and did not have a German teachers' license, but I realized that I did not need one to open my own tutoring service. I did it. As you can see, I am writing. I ask you the same question. What do you have in your hand? The prophet asked the widow woman the question, "What do you have in your house?" My friend, use what you have. There are resources all around you; they are at your disposal.

"The slothful man hideth his hand in his bosom, and will not so much as bring it to his mouth again." Proverbs 19:24.

Let us pray together:

Father, in Jesus name, help me not to be lazy or afraid. Help me to remember that You will supply all of my needs according to Your riches not mine. Help me to take the limits off of You. I receive, in Jesus name.

Chapter 4
Use What You Have (Verse 10)

Philippians 4:13 *"I can do all things through Christ which strengtheneth me."*

Now that you see what you have available, use it, do it. Do not just say, *"I can do all things."* Go out and *do* those things. Don't just talk about what you want to do, think you should do or are going to do. Do it! Do it, do it, do it, do it, and do it now! I Timothy 1:12 says, *"And I thank Christ Jesus our Lord, who hath enabled me, for that he counted me faithful, putting me into the ministry."* You have been enabled.

In Acts 3:6, when Peter and John saw the man and knew what he needed and what they could do, they did. They spoke the Word with confidence and that which they commanded, in word, came to pass. They did not just say, *"We have the power."* They actually used their power. It was given to them by God to *use* it. They did not even have to pray about it. Sometimes, we waste a lot of time or make excuses while waiting and even saying we are praying about what God is waiting on us to *DO*. Do not waste time worrying about what you do not have. Focus on what you do have and *use* it.

Read II Corinthians 9:12 and I Peter 4:10, 11

II Corinthians 9:12

"For the administration of this service not only supplieth the want of the saints, but is abundant also by many thanksgivings unto God."

I Peter 4:10, 11

"As every man hath received the gift, even so minister the same one to another, as good stewards of the manifold grace of God. If any man speak, let him speak as the oracles of God; if any man minister, let him do it as of the ability which God giveth: that God in all things may be glorified through Jesus Christ, to whom be praise and dominion for ever and ever. Amen."

Chapter 5

Seek Instructions Every Step of the Way

(Verses 12-14)

Genesis 24: 12 - 14

12 And he said, O Lord God of my master Abraham, I pray thee, send me good speed this day, and shew kindness unto my master Abraham.

13 Behold, I stand here by the well of water; and the daughters of the men of the city come out to draw water:

14 And let it come to pass, that the damsel to whom I shall say, Let down thy pitcher I pray thee, that I may drink; and she shall say, Drink, and I will give thy camels drink also: let the same be she that thou hast appointed for thy servant Isaac; and thereby shall I know that thou hast shewed kindness unto my master.

This servant had received instructions from Abraham, his master, and had left. As he is on the way, he is prayerful. We must always pray. More than any man, it is the Lord who knows our way and He is the one who will make our way prosperous. Proverbs 3:5-6, 5:21, 12:1.

Proverbs 3:5-6

5 Trust in the LORD with all thine heart; and lean not unto thine own understanding.

6 In all thy ways acknowledge him, and he shall direct thy paths.

Proverbs 5:21

For the ways of man are before the eyes of the LORD, and he pondereth all his goings.

Proverbs 12:1

Whoso loveth instruction loveth knowledge: but he that hateth reproof is brutish.

Proverbs 8:10-21

10 Receive my instruction, and not silver; and knowledge rather than choice gold.

11 For wisdom is better than rubies; and all the things that may be desired are not to be compared to it.

12 I wisdom dwell with prudence, and find out knowledge of witty inventions.

13 The fear of the LORD is to hate evil: pride, and arrogancy, and the evil way, and the forward mouth, do I hate.

14 Counsel is mine, and sound wisdom: I am understanding; I have strength.

15 By me kings reign, and princes decree justice.

16 By me princes rule, and nobles, even all judges of the earth.

17 I love them that love me; and those that seek me early shall find me.

18 Riches and honour are with me; yea, durable riches and righteousness.

19 My fruit is better than gold, yea, than fine gold; and my revenue than choice silver.

20 I lead in the way of righteousness, in the midst of the paths of judgment.

21 That I may cause those that love me to inherit substance; and I will fill their treasures.

Proverbs 2:1-9

1 My son, if thou wilt receive my words, and hide my commandments with thee;

2 So that thou incline thine ear unto wisdom, and apply thine heart to understanding;

3 Yea, if thou criest after knowledge, and liftest up thy voice for understanding;

4 If thou seekest her as silver, and searchest for her as for hid treasures;

5 Then shalt thou understand the fear of the LORD, and find the knowledge of God.

6 For the LORD giveth wisdom; out of his mouth cometh knowledge and understanding.

7 He layeth up sound wisdom for the righteous: he is a buckler to them that walk uprightly.

8 He keepeth the paths of judgment, and preserveth the way of his saints.

9 Then shalt thou understand righteousness, and judgment, and equity; yea, every good path.

I ask the Lord to put people around you who will advise you well. Don't be like Rehoboam.

I Kings 12:1-16

1And Rehoboam went to Shechem: for all Israel were come to Shechem to make him king.

2 And it came to pass, when Jeroboam the son of Nebat, who was yet in Egypt, heard of it, (for he was fled from the presence of king Solomon, and Jeroboam dwelt in Egypt;)

3 That they sent and called him. And Jeroboam and all the congregation of Israel came, and spake unto Rehoboam, saying,

4 Thy father made our yoke grievous: now therefore make thou the grievous service of thy father, and his heavy yoke which he put upon us, lighter, and we will serve thee.

5 *And he said unto them, Depart yet for three days, then come again to me. And the people departed.*

6 *And king Rehoboam consulted with the old men, that stood before Solomon his father while he yet lived, and said, How do ye advise that I may answer this people?*

7 *And they spake unto him, saying, If thou wilt be a servant unto this people this day, and wilt serve them, and answer them, and speak good words to them, then they will be thy servants for ever.*

8 *But he forsook the counsel of the old men, which they had given him, and consulted with the young men that were grown up with him, and which stood before him:*

9 *And he said unto them, What counsel give ye that we may answer this people, who have spoken to me, saying, Make the yoke which thy father did put upon us lighter?*

10 *And the young men that were grown up with him spake unto him, saying, Thus shalt thou speak unto this people that spake unto thee, saying, Thy father made our yoke heavy, but make thou it lighter unto us; thus shalt thou say unto them, My little finger shall be thicker than my father's loins.*

11 *And now whereas my father did lade you with a heavy yoke, I will add to your yoke: my father hath chastised you with whips, but I will chastise you with scorpions.*

12 *So Jeroboam and all the people came to Rehoboam the third day, as the king had appointed, saying, Come to me again the third day.*

13 *And the king answered the people roughly, and forsook the old men's counsel that they gave him;*

14 *And spake to them after the counsel of the young men, saying, My father made your yoke heavy, and I will add to your yoke: my father also chastised you with whips, but I will chastise you with scorpions.*

15 *Wherefore the king hearkened not unto the people; for the cause was from the LORD, that he might perform his saying, which the LORD spake by Ahijah the Shilonite unto Jeroboam the son of Nebat.*

16 So when all Israel saw that the king hearkened not unto them, the people answered the king, saying, What portion have we in David? neither have we inheritance in the son of Jesse: to your tents, O Israel: now see to thine own house, David. So Israel departed unto their tents.

As you seek Him and make every move carefully, the Lord will instruct you and clarify confusing things. He will cause you to be creative. He will give you new ideas (Proverbs 8:12) and enable you to do what you need to do.

Go ahead. Seek Him, He will be found. Pray. Pray. Pray.

Chapter 6

Know that God Will Provide. Trust God.

(Verse 15)

Genesis 24:15 *"And it came to pass, before he had done speaking, that, behold, Rebekah came out, who was born to Bethuel, son of Milcah, the wife of Nahor, Abraham's brother, with her pitcher upon her shoulder."*

The Lord allowed Rebekah to show up right at the time when she was supposed to. She was neither early or late. Just like the ram in the bush, when Abraham was on Mt. Moriah with Isaac. Abraham was sure God would provide. He provided the ram, not too early, not too late. God is a Provider and He will provide for you if you trust Him.

Genesis 22:7-14

7 And Isaac spake unto Abraham his father, and said, My father: and he said, Here am I, my son. And he said, Behold the fire and the wood: but where is the lamb for a burnt offering?

8 And Abraham said, My son, God will provide himself a lamb for a burnt offering: so they went both of them together.

9 And they came to the place which God had told him of; and Abraham built an altar there, and laid the wood in order, and bound Isaac his son, and laid him on the altar upon the wood.

10 *And Abraham stretched forth his hand, and took the knife to slay his son.*

11 *And the angel of the LORD called unto him out of heaven, and said, Abraham, Abraham: and he said, Here am I.*

12 *And he said, Lay not thine hand upon the lad, neither do thou any thing unto him: for now I know that thou fearest God, seeing thou hast not withheld thy son, thine only son from me.*

13 *And Abraham lifted up his eyes, and looked, and behold behind him a ram caught in a thicket by his horns: and Abraham went and took the ram, and offered him up for a burnt offering in the stead of his son.*

14 *And Abraham called the name of that place Jehovah-jireh: as it is said to this day, In the mount of the LORD it shall be seen.*

He is your Jehovah-jireh, the Lord who provides.

Psalm 23:1 says, "*The LORD is my shepherd; I shall not want.*" The Psalmist was expressing his dependence on and confidence in the Lord who was his Shepherd. Imagine trusting God to the point that you are able to confidently say, "I shall not want" or "I shall not be in want" or "I shall not lack." There is no lack in God. He is a God of abundance. Psalm 36,7-8 says, "*How excellent is thy lovingkindness, O God! therefore the children of men put their trust under the shadow of thy wings. They shall be abundantly satisfied with the fatness of thy house; and thou shalt make them drink of the river of thy pleasures.*" Ephesians 3:20 says, "*Now unto him that is able to do exceeding abundantly above all that we ask or think, according to the power that worketh in us.*" Throughout the rest of Psalm 23,

David details God's providence. The green pastures of verse 2 are an indication of the Lord putting us in prosperous situations. They are green and flourishing. The still waters show us that, sometimes, He will cause us to experience still, smooth, and peaceful times; it is God's providence. He restores us when we feel worn out or discouraged. If our joy or peace has been taken away, He will restore these unto us; it is part of His providence. Even if we end up going "*through the valley of the shadow of death*", there is no reason to fear for He is ever with us. He will comfort us during these times and we will surely *pass* through them and not stay in them. We, God's people, always 'pass through' these times. Glory, Hallelujah, what a Provider He is!

Look at Psalm 31:19, 68:10, and Philippians 4:19

Psalm 31:19

Oh how great is thy goodness, which thou hast laid up for them that fear thee; which thou hast wrought for them that trust in thee before the sons of men!

Psalm 68:10

Thy congregation hath dwelt therein: thou, O God, hast prepared of thy goodness for the poor.

Philippians 4:19

But my God shall supply all your need according to his riches in glory by Christ Jesus.

When you allow the vision you are pursuing to have a God-ordained, God-led, God-inspired vision. You can be sure that He will provide all the resources necessary to bring it all to pass. He will provide people, money, places, opportunities, ideas, strength and all the guidance necessary to bring His vision to pass through you. It is God's great desire that we prosper on every level. When I say 'every level' I mean, every level. Whether the vision is a small personal desire or a big ministry goal involving hundreds or thousands, it is all the same to God. He wants us to prosper, therefore He helps us. If we would trust Him and obey Him, '*He will withhold NO GOOD THING from US* (Psalms 84:11)'.

Psalm 35:27; Jeremiah 32:40-41; Psalm 84:11; 3 John 2

Psalms 35:27

27 Let them shout for joy, and be glad, that favour my righteous cause: yea, let them say continually, Let the Lord be magnified, which hath pleasure in the prosperity of his servant.

Jeremiah 32: 40-41

40 And I will make an everlasting covenant with them, that I will not turn away from them, to do them good; but I will put my fear in their hearts, that they shall not depart from me.

41 Yea, I will rejoice over them to do them good, and I will plant them in this land assuredly with my whole heart and with my whole soul.

Psalm 84:11

11 For the Lord God is a sun and shield: the Lord will give grace and glory: no good thing will he withhold from them that walk uprightly.

3 John 2

2 Beloved, I wish above all things that thou mayest prosper and be in health, even as thy soul prospereth.

Chapter 7
Expect Divine Meetings and Visitations

In verse 27 the servant said, *"Blessed be the LORD God of my master Abraham, who hath not left destitute my master of his mercy and his truth: I being in the way, the LORD led me to the house of my master's brethren."* He acknowledges here that it was the Lord Who provided this divine meeting. Remember, at this point, the servant did not have a street name, house number, or telephone number. It had to have been God. Chapters 6 and 7 are very similar. Here, again, you will see the LORD God provide supernaturally. This meeting was not planned by man and it was not an accident. It was the provision of Almighty God and this is what we should expect when we are on assignment or in pursuit of a vision.

In I Kings 17:10, we see another divine meeting. God told Elijah to go to the city of Zarephath. He told Elijah that He had already commanded *a woman* to take care of him there. Again, no name or street or house number. The man of God expected the Lord to provide by doing what He promised. The Bible says, in verse 10, *"So he arose and went to Zarephath. And when he came to the gate of the city, behold, the widow woman was there gathering of sticks: and he called to her, and said, Fetch me, I pray thee, a little water in a vessel, that I may drink."* Imagine that! When he got to the gate of the city, *the woman* just happened to be there gathering sticks. This was truly a divine meeting.

Another event is found in Acts 10, when Cornelius was praying to God. He had a vision and an angel of God instructed him to send for Peter. He believed God's Word and sent his servants. By the time the servant got to Peter, the Lord had already prepared him for the "meeting". The servants found him where the Lord said they would and Peter was ready to return to Cornelius with them. We must expect this of the Lord even today. We must expect Him to cause us to meet those we should. We must expect to divinely run into people who can and will add to us and help us to fulfill our destiny. Why not believe, isn't God the same yesterday, today and forever? Live in expectation. Everyday is important. Do not limit God. Your day of visitation could be today.

Chapter 8
Your Gift Will Make Room For You

Abraham's servant had brought gifts with him. Verse 30 said, when Laban, her brother, *saw* the earring and bracelets on his sister's hand, and when he heard the words, he told the man to, *"Come in, thou blessed of the LORD; wherefore standest thou without?"* (24:31). I can imagine that he was very impressed with the wealth of Abraham's servant.

We also have gifts. We have gifts and talents that the Lord can use to make an impression on those who need to add to us. Do not be ashamed to use your gifts whatever they may be, for the Lord has supplied you with them for a reason. You should also develop your gifts, as you do this, you will position yourself for bigger and greater doors to open.

A side note: The giving of a gift should be just that, giving. The Bible says if we give, it shall be given unto us. What shall be given unto us? That which we have given and more. We should not only give to get, or give to impress or give to bribe, we should simply give. God loves a cheerful givers, not givers with ulterior motives. He is looking for givers. We must however, have what is necessary to give. We cannot give what we do not have. That is God's department. He gives us what we need to give. Our God supplies. Whether it is through a talent, gold, silver, money or by some other means. Our God supplies. As we gratefully acknowledge the fact that He is our source, we can also humbly utilize that which He has supplied. Go ahead, use your gift. It will make room or open doors for you. And do not forget, big or small, use what *you* have. I think of a sports team. You are on the team because you can play and you are good, though there might be some who are better. You might be on the bench often because there are those who are better, but the fact is you are still on the team and they need you even on the bench. You help to make-up the team, your presence is important. Read 1 Sam. 30:1-31. You will be greatly blessed. Again, be who God has made you to be. Use your gift:

I Samuel 30:1-31

1 *And it came to pass, when David and his men were come to Ziklag on the third day, that the Amalekites had invaded the south, and Ziklag, and smitten Ziklag, and burned it with fire;*

2 *And had taken the women captives, that were therein: they slew not any, either great or small, but carried them away, and went on their way.*

3 *So David and his men came to the city, and, behold, it was burned with fire; and their wives, and their sons, and their daughters, were taken captives.*

4 *Then David and the people that were with him lifted up their voice and wept, until they had no more power to weep.*

5 *And David's two wives were taken captives, Ahinoam the Jezreelitess, and Abigail the wife of Nabal the Carmelite.*

6 *And David was greatly distressed; for the people spake of stoning him, because the soul of all the people was grieved, every man for his sons and for his daughters: but David encouraged himself in the Lord his God.*

7 And David said to Abiathar the priest, Ahimelech's son, I pray thee, bring me hither the ephod. And Abiathar brought thither the ephod to David.

8 And David enquired at the Lord, saying, Shall I pursue after this troop? shall I overtake them? And he answered him, Pursue: for thou shalt surely overtake them, and without fail recover all.

9 So David went, he and the six hundred men that were with him, and came to the brook Besor, where those that were left behind stayed.

10 But David pursued, he and four hundred men: for two hundred abode behind, which were so faint that they could not go over the brook Besor.

11 And they found an Egyptian in the field, and brought him to David, and gave him bread, and he did eat; and they made him drink water;

12 And they gave him a piece of a cake of figs, and two clusters of raisins: and when he had eaten, his spirit came again to him: for he had eaten no bread, nor drunk any water, three days and three nights.

13 And David said unto him, To whom belongest thou? and whence art thou? And he said, I am a young man of Egypt, servant to an Amalekite; and my master left me, because three days agone I fell sick.

14 We made an invasion upon the south of the Cherethites, and upon the coast which belongeth to Judah, and upon the south of Caleb; and we burned Ziklag with fire.

15 And David said to him, Canst thou bring me down to this company? And he said, Swear unto me by God, that thou wilt neither kill me, nor deliver me into the hands of my master, and I will bring thee down to this company.

16 And when he had brought him down, behold, they were spread abroad upon all the earth, eating and drinking, and dancing, because of all the great spoil that they had taken out of the land of the Philistines, and out of the land of Judah.

17 And David smote them from the twilight even unto the evening of the next day: and there escaped not a man of them, save four hundred young men, which rode upon camels, and fled.

18 And David recovered all that the Amalekites had carried away: and David rescued his two wives.

19 And there was nothing lacking to them, neither small nor great, neither sons nor daughters, neither spoil, nor any thing that they had taken to them: David recovered all.

20 And David took all the flocks and the herds, which they drave before those other cattle, and said, This is David's spoil.

21 And David came to the two hundred men, which were so faint that they could not follow David, whom they had made also to abide at the brook Besor: and they went forth to meet David, and to meet the people that were with him: and when David came near to the people, he saluted them.

22 Then answered all the wicked men and men of Belial, of those that went with David, and said, Because they went not with us, we will not give them ought of the spoil that we have recovered, save to every man his wife and his children, that they may lead them away, and depart.

23 Then said David, Ye shall not do so, my brethren, with that which the Lord hath given us, who hath preserved us, and delivered the company that came against us into our hand.

24 For who will hearken unto you in this matter? but as his part is that goeth down to the battle, so shall his part be that tarrieth by the stuff: they shall part alike.

25 And it was so from that day forward, that he made it a statute and an ordinance for Israel unto this day.

26 And when David came to Ziklag, he sent of the spoil unto the elders of Judah, even to his friends, saying, Behold a present for you of the spoil of the enemies of the Lord;

27 To them which were in Bethel, and to them which were in south Ramoth, and to them which were in Jattir,

28 *And to them which were in Aroer, and to them which were in Siphmoth, and to them which were in Eshtemoa,*

29 *And to them which were in Rachal, and to them which were in the cities of the Jerahmeelites, and to them which were in the cities of the Kenites,*

30 *And to them which were in Hormah, and to them which were in Chorashan, and to them which were in Athach,*

31 *And to them which were in Hebron, and to all the places where David himself and his men were wont to haunt.*

Chapter 9

"First Things First. Stay Focused."

In verse 33, the servant refused to eat before stating his business. We must learn how to prioritize if we are going to accomplish anything great. Ecclesiastes 3:11 tells us that there is a time for everything. Do not play when you should be praying. Do not take on a phone call when you should be reading your Bible. Do not sleep when you should be meditating. Do not put off for tomorrow what you should be doing today. Do not waste time when there is so much work to be done. Do God's business when you should and man's business when it is time. Do what you must do, when you must and what you can do, when you can do it. Whatever you do, do not say, "I'll do it whenever I get around to it." Do it and do it when it is time, and that time is probably *now*. So many saints and others take treasures (gifts, talents, inventions, and creative ideas) to the grave. They were busy doing one thing or another and just never got around to doing what they really <u>wanted</u> to do.

Do not be distracted. Do not begin to do something and then stop in the middle and get too busy on something else instead of doing what you really should be doing. Stay focused. Ask yourself, "What am I doing here?" Answer your own question and then do the answer.

Look out for time wasters: people or things that come to waste your time. Tell that person on the telephone, "I've got to go..." Tell them, "We'll have lunch later." Do not allow people to plan wasting your time. A lunch date here, a dinner there and you will find hours and hours spent not accomplishing much of anything, just wasting time. Don't do it. Even if you go to lunch, go on purpose. Why am I here? If it is for fun then have fun, but don't waste time. Do what you are supposed to do when you are supposed to do it. First things first.

Chapter 10
Give God The Glory

From verse 35 to verse 52, we see how the servant constantly gives the glory or credit for every breakthrough to the God of his master Abraham. We must do the same. Give God the glory! Give God HIS glory! It is all His. Before the door is open, thank God. While the door is in the process of opening, thank God. After the door has been opened and you can see the manifestation of your dream, thank God. Thank Him all through the process. Recognize that all of what is happening to you is only because of and through Him. Give God the glory. In II Samuel 6:12-23, the Bible says that when David had gone only six paces he would stop and sacrifice.

II Samuel 6:12-23

12 *And it was told king David, saying, The LORD hath blessed the house of Obededom, and all that pertaineth unto him, because of the ark of God. So David went and brought up the ark of God from the house of Obededom into the city of David with gladness.*

13 *And it was so, that when they that bare the ark of the LORD had gone six paces, he sacrificed oxen and fatlings.*

14 *And David danced before the LORD with all his might; and David was girded with a linen ephod.*

15 *So David and all the house of Israel brought up the ark of the LORD with shouting, and with the sound of the trumpet.*

16 *And as the ark of the LORD came into the city of David, Michal Saul's daughter looked through a window, and saw king David leaping and dancing before the LORD; and she despised him in her heart.*

17 *And they brought in the ark of the LORD, and set it in his place, in the midst of the tabernacle that David had pitched for it: and David offered burnt offerings and peace offerings before the LORD.*

18 *And as soon as David had made an end of offering burnt offerings and peace offerings, he blessed the people in the name of the LORD of hosts.*

19 *And he dealt among all the people, even among the whole multitude of Israel, as well to the women as men, to every one a cake of bread, and a good piece of flesh, and a flagon of wine. So all the people departed every one to his house.*

20 *Then David returned to bless his household. And Michal the daughter of Saul came out to meet David, and said, How glorious was the king of Israel today, who uncovered himself to day in the eyes of the handmaids of his servants, as one of the vain fellows shamelessly uncovereth himself!*

21 *And David said unto Michal, It was before the LORD, which chose me before thy father, and before all his house, to appoint me ruler over the people of the LORD, over Israel: therefore will I play before the LORD.*

22 *And I will yet be more vile than thus, and will be base in mine own sight: and of the maidservants which thou hast spoken of, of them shall I be had in honour.*

23 *Therefore Michal the daughter of Saul had no child unto the day of her death.*

This is a good lesson for us. Stop often and give God the glory. Thank Him. Praise Him. Testify about Him. Do not speak the

problem, speak the solution: "It looks like this but my God will..."
Give Him the glory. It is all His.

Psalm 112: 1-10

1 *Praise ye the LORD. Blessed is the man that feareth the LORD, that delighteth greatly in his commandments.*

2 *His seed shall be mighty upon earth: the generation of the upright shall be blessed.*

3 *Wealth and riches shall be in his house: and his righteousness endureth for ever.*

4 *Unto the upright there ariseth light in the darkness: he is gracious, and full of compassion, and righteous.*

5 *A good man sheweth favour, and lendeth: he will guide his affairs with discretion.*

6 *Surely he shall not be moved for ever: the righteous shall be in everlasting remembrance.*

7 *He shall not be afraid of evil tidings: his heart is fixed, trusting in the LORD.*

8 *His heart is established, he shall not be afraid, until he see his desire upon his enemies.*

9 *He hath dispersed, he hath given to the poor; his righteousness endureth for ever; hi shorn shall be exalted with honour.*

10 *The wicked shall see it, and be grieved; he shall gnash with his teeth, and melt away: the desire of the wicked shall perish.*

Psalm 113:1-9

1 *Praise ye the LORD. Praise, O ye servants of the LORD, praise the name of the LORD.*

2 *Blessed be the name of the LORD from this time forth and for evermore.*

3 *From the rising of the sun unto the going down of the same the LORD'S name is to be praised.*

4 *The LORD is high above all nations, and his glory above the heavens.*

41

5 *Who is like unto the* L*ORD* *our God, who dwelleth on high,*

6 *Who humbleth himself to behold the things that are in heaven, and in the earth!*

7 *He raiseth up the poor out of the dust, and lifteth the needy out of the dunghill;*

8 *That he may set him with princes, even with the princes of his people.*

9 *He maketh the barren woman to keep house, and to be a joyful mother of children. Praise ye the* L*ORD*.

Meet the Author

Dr. Annmarie McQueen is a woman of prayer whom God has called to the Kingdom for such a time as this.

She is married to Dist. Elder Michael C. McQueen, Sr. They have three wonderful children, Michelle, Michael, Jr., and Miguel. The family lived on the mission field in Germany for over twenty years where they pastored Faith Ministries International church. Dr. McQueen is the Assistant to the Bishop of the European Council of Nations East.

Dr. McQueen is a Preacher and Teacher of the Word of the Lord. She has preached the Word of God throughout Europe, in Africa and the United States. God has used his Word through her to touch lives in such places as Egypt, Korea, Singapore, Ghana, Nigeria, Croatia and more.

As the Prayer General and worship leader for the European Council of Nations of the Pentecostal Assemblies of the World for many years, Dr. Annmarie has experienced ministry from many sides. She has been seen on religious programming for television in New York and parts of Texas, on the radio in various states as well as in publications such as The Crusader, a Germany-based military newspaper and The Church. She is the author of five books and scores of magazine articles. She is the founder of McQueen Universal Ministries (MUM), the Making a Difference Conferences and the Mantle Wearers Conferences for leaders. She holds degrees in Science, Mathematics and Education. She is a certified Life Coach and sits on the Board of The Life Catalyst Coaching Organization for Life Coach Certification. The MUM headquarters building is located in Fort Worth, Texas where she runs the Prayer and Training Center.

McQueen Universal Ministries, Inc.

P.O. Box 34082 ~ Fort Worth, TX 76162-4082, U.S.A. ~ 001-817-715-4606 ~ mcqueenum@gmail.com ~ www.mcqueenum.org

www.ingramcontent.com/pod-product-compliance
Lightning Source LLC
Chambersburg PA
CBHW022347040426
42449CB00006B/764